LIFE IS FULL:

Musings on the Beauty of Life, Growth, and Love

By
Cassandra N. Vincent

Life is Full: Musings on the Beauty of Life, Growth, and Love by Cassandra N. Vincent, Vincent Media & Consulting, LLC Publishing Services, Baltimore, MD.

www.cassandranvincent.com

© 2019 Cassandra N. Vincent | Vincent Media & Consulting, LLC

All rights reserved. No portion of this book may be reproduced in any form without permission from the publisher, except as permitted by U.S. copyright law. For permissions contact:

info@cassandranvincent.com

Cover and eBook design by Vincent Media & Consulting, LLC.

ISBN-13: 978-0-578-51923-4

Disclaimer:

The author of this book does not provide medical advice or prescribe the use of any technique as a form of medical treatment for physical, emotional, or medical problems without the advice of a physician, either directly or indirectly. The intent of the author is to only provide information of a general nature to help in your quest for personal and spiritual development. In the event you use any of the information in this book for yourself, which is your constitutional right, the author assumes no liability for your actions.

Acknowledgements

To every soul that needs refreshing and has a longing for fuller moments in life. To my father and mother, Wallace and Joyce Vincent for coming together and creating a blessed family and a beautiful legacy. To my siblings, Quinton, Jenee', Gabrielle, and Paul for supporting my growth and for your love. To my niece, Shondraiya for your courage and beautiful intelligence beyond your years—you are a gift. To my nephews, Aires and Jonah you are blessed. To my mentees for teaching me so much and for giving me an opportunity to serve young women who are a reflection of me.

Contents

Acknowledgements iv

Introduction vii

One | The Beauty Of Life 1

Two | The Beauty Of Growth 31

Three | The Beauty Of Love 103

Closing Reflections 137

About The Author 141

About The Book 143

Introduction

There are times in life when pauses are required to reflect upon the sum of your life. In these times, depending upon your life experiences, you may feel a number of emotions, hopeful, excited, or perhaps you feel numb to it all. Life is like one big journey that has parts and people in it that are constantly in motion. When you take time to reflect on your life's journey -- how do you describe life? If you could sum up all of your days up to this point, what do you think about your life and where you are heading? What is the story of your life? Are you grateful or hopeful? Or is life dragging from one chapter to the next? The question we have to consistently answer with our time and our decisions is: "Am I truly living and fulfilling my purpose?

Life Is Full: Musings on Life, Growth, and Love takes a look at lessons learned and encourages love and personal growth. When we take time to evaluate where we are we can better navigate where we are heading in life. Reflecting upon life from a place of gratitude, can provide us with a positive outlook. Our lives are filled with so many experiences from birth, through adolescence and adulthood that sometimes our outlook on life and how God intended for us to experience it can become skewed. We should be careful to push against accepting the hardships of life to become the definition of our life.

In our comings and goings, we often come across others who have an humdrum approach to life and we find others who seem to have passion and vigor for it. As an observer and lover of life, these two vastly different approaches causes you to question what drives the two types of people to view life as they do. Further reflection makes you look more deeply at which of the two you are. Triumphs and challenges are common to us all. We each experience the ups and downs of life, however, the person who views life as full is the one who pulls opportunity from their experiences. The fullness of life has much to do with how one views and approaches each day. The fullness of life can be experienced when we extract wisdom from obstacles, possess peace despite circumstances, and thrive in meaningfulness. A full life is quite relative to a full heart. A heart that comprehends life as an adventurous journey of peaks and valleys, but a beautiful journey, is a full heart.

At the writing of this book, I found myself in a conversation that was quite interesting and affirming. One day while substitute teaching a class at a local high school, I filled in for a very well liked teacher. Many of the students referred to this teacher as one of the best in the school and in her absence many of her students stopped by to greet her. Much to their surprise, these students found me, Ms. V., and not their beloved

Ms. S. Well, on this particular day one of her students stopped by and plopped down into a chair beside my chair and we began to chat about why he had decided to retreat to Ms. S's classroom. The student provided me with all of the reasons why his current class and teacher frustrated him to the point of walking down to the classroom I was covering. After engaging him a bit more about his decision to leave his assigned class, there was a slight pause and then randomly, the student blurts out, "*Man life is hard*!". I quietly giggled to myself wondering why he had arrived at this conclusion, but on a more serious note wanted to know his reasoning. The student went on to explain his experience as a young, black, male teenager and some of the struggles he had been experiencing for several years now. He shared how different some of his classmates' lives were from his. And he shared how he wanted to help support his family face their financial needs. Finally, one of the concerns that was striking and no joking matter was that of his concerns for returning the next school year and surviving, what he described as, a dangerous summer. This student lived in inner city Baltimore and attended school in one of the neighboring counties, and to some considered slightly better schooling.

Although, I was taken aback by the young man's statement I quickly investigated, with questions, his feelings for thinking that life was hard at such a young age. As he went onto to describe the challenges, I attempted to better understand some of his experiences. What he described is absolutely an harsh reality. When you are fearful that you will not live, through the summer, to see your junior year of high school, is absolutely a hard thing for many to even fathom. This young man's experience is not uncommon and if you have lived any amount of time and have experienced some form of challenge or hardship. We will face challenges that seem so hard and so unbearable but we must insist that this will not be the theme of our lives.

After speaking to this student further, I wondered what positive male role models in my network might be a fit for connecting the young man to be possibly mentored. The student's story moved me. It is one that is shared by many other young, black, males. Facing this harsh reality does make life hard. Later that day, I happened to meet one of the coaches for the school. I briefly shared my conversation with the coach in hopes that I could refer this student to him for mentoring. What I discovered is that the student was a very bright and smart kid, according to the coach. This same student was once an excellent basketball player for the school. However, this same student had decided to choose other activities that were proving to be counterproductive to him being able to play for the school. The student was prioritizing unhealthy behaviors and relationships above his dreams of playing basketball which in many ways could lead to opportunities and relationships that could be life-changing.

I share this story and interaction, because this student is like many people -- aware of what life is but sometimes unwilling or unknowingly not changing patterns in our lives to create better. Like this young man, many people are staring opportunity and their life-changing moments right in the face. How often do we decide to remain the same and not make the changes we know we need to change our lives? Sometimes we are unwilling and other times perhaps we just do not know where to start. What is certain is that we must be active participants in creating a life we desire to experience. It will not just happen. To experience a full life we must be proactive in making those changes a priority.

Whether we are sixteen or sixty, decisions, discovery, and doing something different will be required to experience a fulfilling life and one of meaning and purpose. However, you define a fulfilled life will require these things to be at play. We have to be open to discovering new things and discovering what brings joy into our lives. We have to consistently make decisions that create a life of peace as well as unlock our potential to reach higher levels of living. A full life will also call for us to do something differently at times. There are times when approaching life with a fresh and new perspective will be required. Living a fulfilled life will require you to do something different to get a different and better outcome.

We can learn a lot from this young man's thoughts on life and his current decisions. If we are honest, we may see a bit of ourselves in him. Too often we set our focus on the hardships and not on all of the possibilities. For many, our actions lead us to repeat the same things over and over which result in the things we truly do not desire. The life God desires for each of us is so far beyond what we generally experience. A full life drives us to push against the average and to never settle for less than an abundant life experience.

Life is one big beautiful adventure that includes highs, lows, lessons, and--more than anything--blessings!

For every person ever born, there are days of great joy and days that are filled with challenge. One thing is certain: We each have been divinely created to change the trajectory of our lives as we take hold of who God has made us to be.

The following pages of this book include my musings on life lessons, growth, and love at one of life's pinnacles— and entering the mid-life stage. This stage is where reflection, adjustment, and reinvention happens because many lessons have been learned and the value of time takes on new meaning. At any point in life, we can discover more of who we are and what it means for the days ahead. Every day counts and is abundantly purposeful. It is our duty to discover what each day holds and to decide how we are going to show up in every moment. This book covers a sample of takeaways from some of my most trying moments and some of my most hopeful and highest moments. The beauty of life is truly becoming aware of the beauty of God and the power in the purpose of your life. Life is full for those who see it as such and those who unlock the meaning behind every moment lived.

If life does not seem beautiful now, it may be an opportunity for you to dig deeper and rediscover your purpose. Life is full and abundant because of the opportunities that we act upon and by what we create out of what has been planted in us by God the greatest creator.

If we are very thoughtful, we can count every valley moment in our lives as times that we have emerged stronger than ever. Like with a garden, we as master gardeners, are gifted time and opportunity to cultivate our lives and grow good things. It is all in how we care for the grounds of our hearts, the time we are granted, and what we decide to plant and uproot along the way. Life indeed is full—full of growth, love, and the beauty of God that can overcome everything we face in life.

When you pursue living a fulfilled and impactful life, you become a lifelong learner embracing growth and daily transformation. A long life of learning unlocks the meanings of moments and experiences that fill our time. As a result, it is important to reflect on what you have learned and put it to use.

These are musings on the beauty of life and the many lessons that have produced wisdom. Taking time to reflect upon life-- embracing its ebbs and flows--helps us determine what we choose for it to become or what it will remain. These musings are personal and in sharing them perhaps others will relate and find solace in their pursuit of living purposefully.

Life is full of what we allow in. Life is full and it is a beautiful opportunity to love, grow, and deeply experience truly living beyond challenges.

The Beauty of Life

ONE
THE BEAUTY OF LIFE

We are born into a world that awaits us with many definitions of who we may or may not become. We are born into families that are filled with love and also with flaws. Our identities are far too often obstructed by outside influences and experiences that challenge our original God-design. From an early age we come into our strong personalities or bold attempts to experience adventure, but slowly--as we journey through time--we either become stronger or our bold attitude diminishes. Life becomes full when we regain the bold and fearless inner young boy or girl who decides to swing upside down on the monkey bars after school. The fullness of our days happens when we are awakened to the absolute greatness inside us. Too often as we grow through adolescence, our brave selves are challenged by what others think and their insecurities. Life becomes full when you get back to that brave self. Life is full when you are reintroduced to who you were always meant to be. When you manage ......a new you a new life." to: When you divorce your insecurities and fears, it is as if you are introduced to a new you and a new life. Life is full when you finally embrace the God-designed you. Boom! The day you divorce every false narrative about yourself and agree with what God says is true about you is when you will truly live. Life becomes abundant in all aspects.

In all, a fulfilled life is one where we never stop growing. We never stop loving. We never stop learning. We take your low points in life and pull out lessons that increase our capacity to triumph over anything we face. The life that is full of blessings is the one in which its possessor fills her days and prioritizes what matters most to her soul's prosperity. The beauty of life is sweet and can be found in one's experiences—both highs and lows. Life is full of God's goodness and is marked with His purpose upon every living creature He designed.

How does the blessed one sum up the days given to her? The happy soul welcomes God's peace into every space she occupies. She views challenges as opportunities to grow. The blessed ones grow from dark moments and overcome them with the light of purpose and love. Life is full of many beautiful things.

There is not one challenge that can overshadow the fullness of life, love, and purpose. The space we have been given to rule in this life comes with an epic master design. Our very image and divine makeup is what speaks to the influence we have over our days and how we live them aloud. How does the blessed one view love, growth, and the beauty of moments granted to her? She rules well over the things, the thoughts, and the activities that fill her days. She is intentional in giving thanks and being filled with gratitude. She views life as an opportunity to be used as God's hand at work in the Earth. The blessed views their days as gifts they give back to God.

Life Is Full: Musings on the Beauty of Life, Growth, and Love

---

Life is like a garden where you grow good things. Life is where good things multiply and continually grow season after season. Life as a well cared for garden produces some of the most beautiful things. The beauty of life is the choices we make to grow our gardens to unimaginable lengths.

The beauty of life is knowing that we have the power and ability to change our life and make it what we want it to be.

Life is what is in your heart, your mind, your soul. Inspect those areas often to see where your heartbeat is for living.

Cultivate and give great attention to your garden.
Otherwise you may be watering the wrong seeds and
ground.

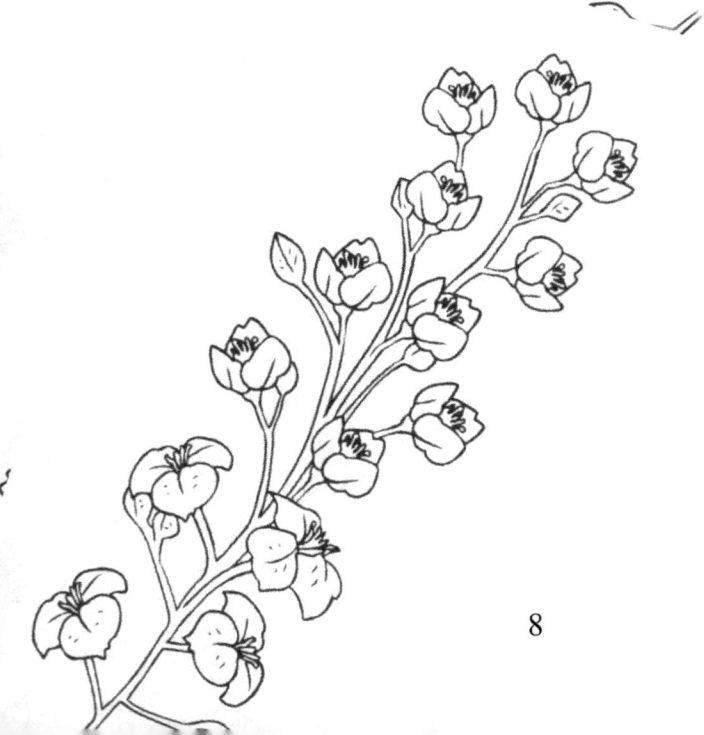

Life is full of beauty, when you consistently seek it in your moments and in your days. The beauty awaiting us in our days is there you have to take time to make note of it and experience it.

Cultivating a life full of joy and happiness is a great undertaking. The journey and joy of happiness is designed for every human soul.

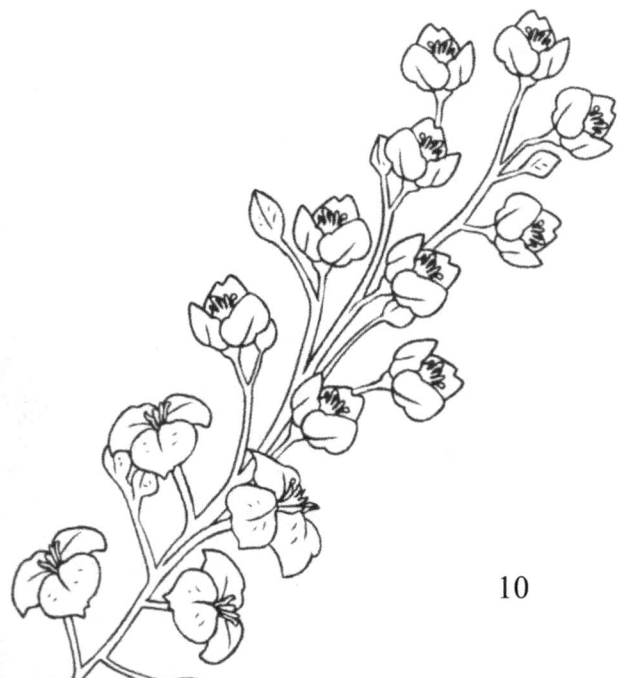

Your happiness, peace, and joy should not be dependent upon another person, however, God designed life for us to enjoy these blessings with others. Enjoy life to the fullest.

Life Is Full: Musings on the Beauty of Life, Growth, and Love

---

Life is full of goodness. Life has challenges, but the goodness of our days can become greater than the challenges. Do not allow a period of trouble to become a lifetime of trouble.

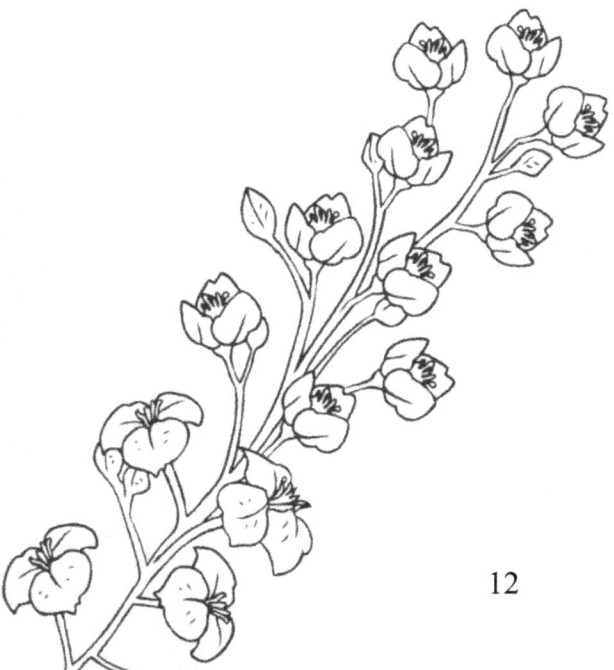

Sometimes the miracle we are looking for is the one inside of us.

Maintain good thoughts and multiply the thoughts you want to come into fruition. We create our life with our words. Our words are what we believe in our hearts. What is in your heart becomes the thing you do and the actions you take.

Life is planting and growing to cultivate ourselves and to have a life that produces a beautiful legacy that reaches generations and generations.

You don't have to tolerate anything that's in conflict with your personal and spiritual growth. Not one thing.

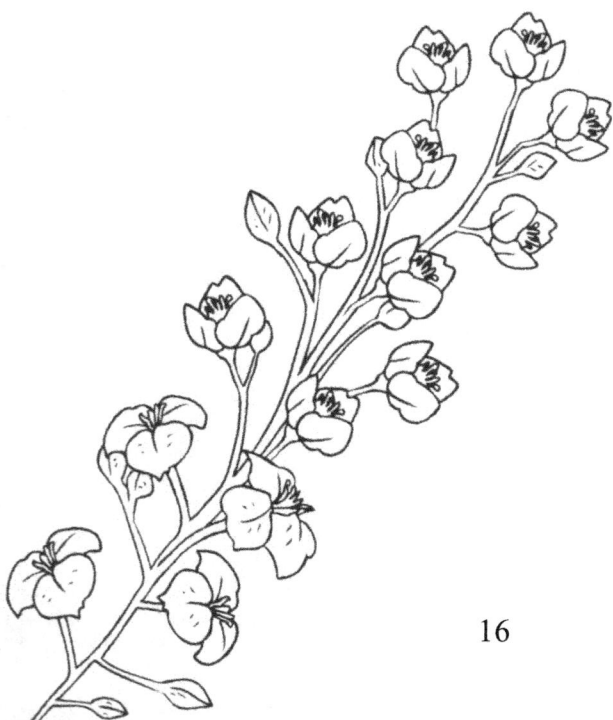

Life is so full and so great. Is life full? How do our days narrate that we are living fulfilled lives? It is not by the fleeting objects that we possess or the fleeting validation that we sometimes seek. A fulfilled life is one that reflects not only the handprints of God but His very image, mind, and heart. When we fill our days with love and His wisdom, life is full. When peace is a priority, life is full.

Life is full of goodness. It is all in how we view what we have been given. It is all in what we decide to do with the blessings we have been given. Life is full.

At times in our journey we question a challenge and the pain that comes with it. With every challenge comes the opportunity for growth. After trouble, we often discover a lesson; challenges can produce strength we did not realize we had, and help us to be grateful for what we may have taken for granted.

Becoming grateful and discovering the importance of being thankful for this life opportunity -- gratitude adds goodness to one's journey. When our days lack gratitude, we fall prey to diminished vision. Foggy vision diminishes our view and grasp of how much we have to celebrate with every moment we experience. A grateful heart quiets the noise of the constant distractions of thanklessness.

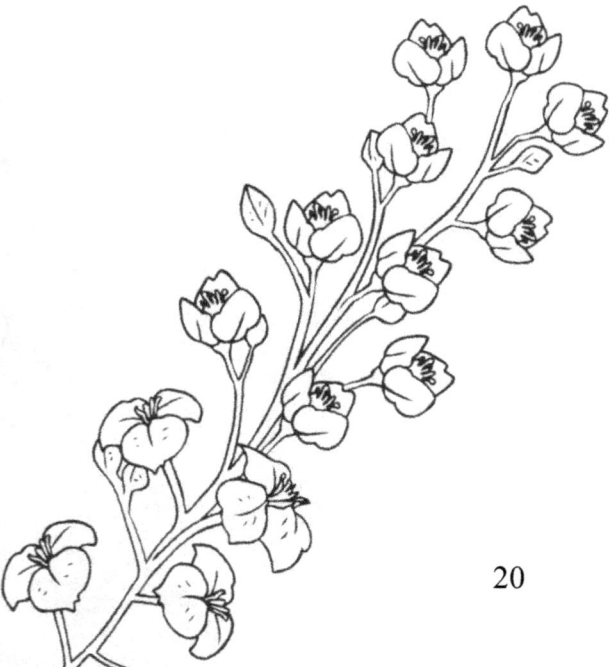

Embrace the current season of your life. Feel it, and uncover all of the blessings tucked inside each day. Each season of your life serves a purpose. We must learn how to live each moment with increasing joy, gratitude, and peacefulness.

Keep your heart pure that is where the good things grow and expand. You may have an off season here or there, but always get back to what is pure. Bitterness eventually becomes a consuming whole. Stay pure.

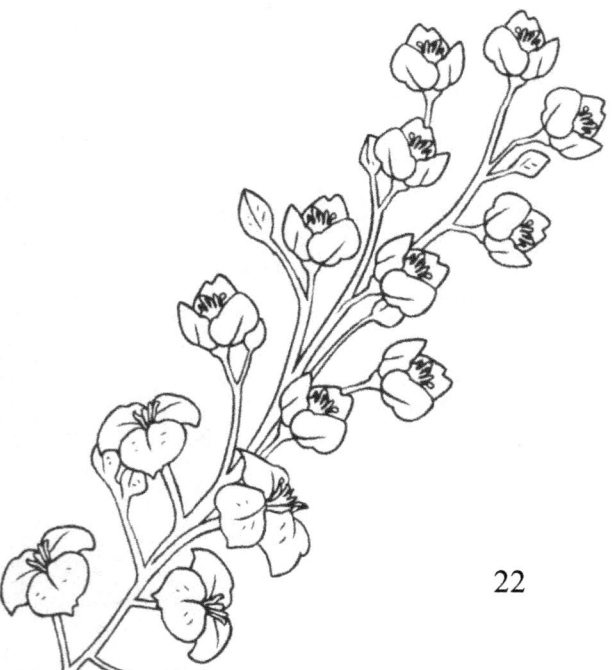

You have the ability to change your world moment by moment of every day.

Each moment and stage of life overflows with opportunities to grow, love, and learn. With every day, come experiences that cause us to take inventory. Life for some seems hopeless. To others, life is full of hope-filled moments. The difference between the two groups is their perspective on the gift of life and their approach to life.

The power to change our lives comes to us every time we speak a word and think a thought. What we say and think soon becomes what we act upon.

In temporary and seemingly dark moments, remember. Even seeds are planted where there is not much light, but something growing underneath is beautiful and needed.

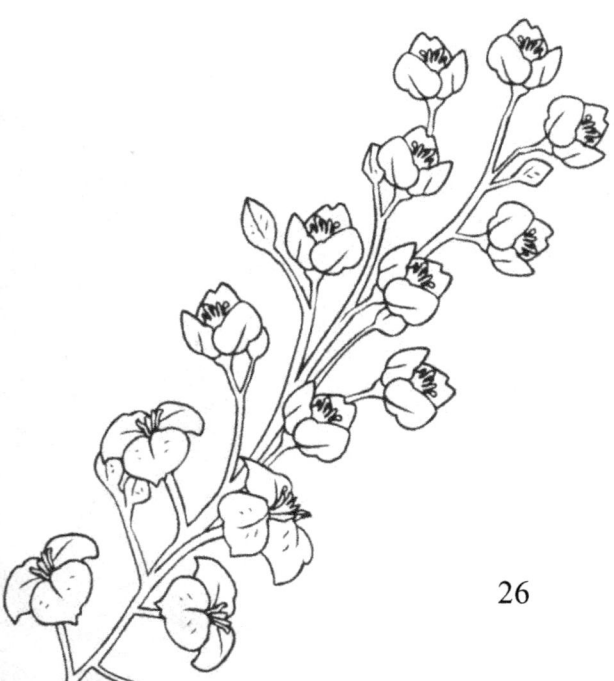

You are purpose. You do not have to find your purpose. You have to discover the path for your life, but purpose is what you were born to be. We are purpose in living form.

Life is full and designed for us to excel at being purpose in living form. We are made in an undeniable image of beauty and creativity. Life is full and awaits those who recognize it.

Like a garden, we as master gardeners, are gifted time and opportunity to cultivate our life's gardens and to grow good things. It is all in how we care for the grounds of our hearts, the time we are granted, and what we decide to plant and uproot along the way. Life indeed is full—full of growth, love, and the beauty of God that can overcome any matter we face.

The Beauty of Growth

TWO
THE BEAUTY OF GROWTH

Life becomes full the moment you prioritize purpose over every minuscule thing that poses a distraction. Life is beautiful. Learning is beautiful. Opportunity for growth and transformation are beautiful. When you take inventory of your days and realize that opportunity exists and that possibility and purpose reside in you, then you unlock life and cultivate a deep appreciation for each day.

The grateful heart reflects on the blessings of this life and refuses to settle into the darkness. This book looks at life's highlights and pulls experience and hope into view based on challenging moments. A celebration of growth and love is described throughout in hopes that every reader is encouraged to continue seeking the good in every moment gifted to us.

Even in life's valleys lies a lesson or wisdom. A full life is having a heart full of thanksgiving and joy for not only what you have overcome in your past, but embracing the present, and not rushing to the future. Life is full of love when you recognize the love that has been extended to you, the love you were created with, the love you are and the love you extend to others. Many abundant reflections come to mind and to the grateful heart that takes hold of constant growth. Life is full of musings on the beauty of life, love, and growth.

You are either growing or remaining the same. There comes a point where remaining the same is too costly and risks us missing the opportunity to live in a big way. Living greatly involves positively impacting your world and the world around you. Remaining the same and limiting your growth, limits your capacity to do great things.

When you become aware of ineffective and unhealthy patterns in your life, you have a choice to improve or ignore what you have become aware of.
To change and improve is to grow.

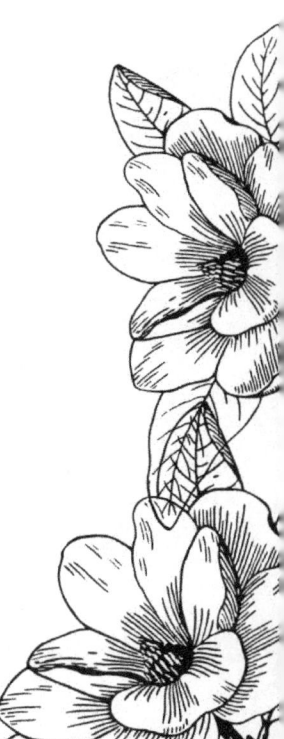

For anything or anyone to grow, careful attention must be given to where you are planted. As a gardener grows things, they pay attention to the other things that grow in the garden. There are other types of roots, weeds, and particularly insects that destroy what is intended to grow and be of good use. Be a good gardner. Take care of your ground, plant good things, and uproot the unnecessary. Cultivate your garden and watch it grow in abundance.

Be mindful of where you are planted, what you are surrounded by, and what should be uprooted in your life, (and heart) that is keeping you from flourishing and growing for a great use.

Do not allow limitations to stifle your vision. Limitations are areas where more questions should be asked; lessons to be learned, and where you need to acknowledge what walls need to be torn down. Limitations are sometimes opportunities to grow beyond the boundaries you may have created in your mind. Push past them and keep growing.

"Feeling stuck" is often a sign that it is time to investigate what needs changing, where you need clarity, and where you may need to release and renew. Stagnancy is a sign that it is time to grow and go. Grow from one stage to the next. Let go of what is out of place and investigate where you are headed next.

Don't be fooled by false confidence; it is deceitful. It is not good to fake it until you make it; rather it is best to become aware of the uniqueness that God has assigned to you.

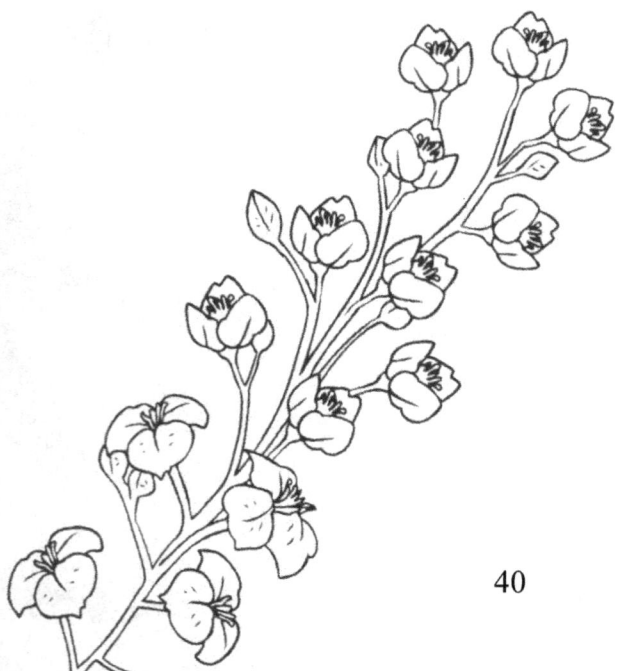

From every single experience, whether good or unfortunate, there is something to be learned. In every experience, we are presented with lessons that teach us something about ourselves, others, or both.

True maturity is evident when you can listen in moments when you do not need to be right and when you do not agree with what is being said.

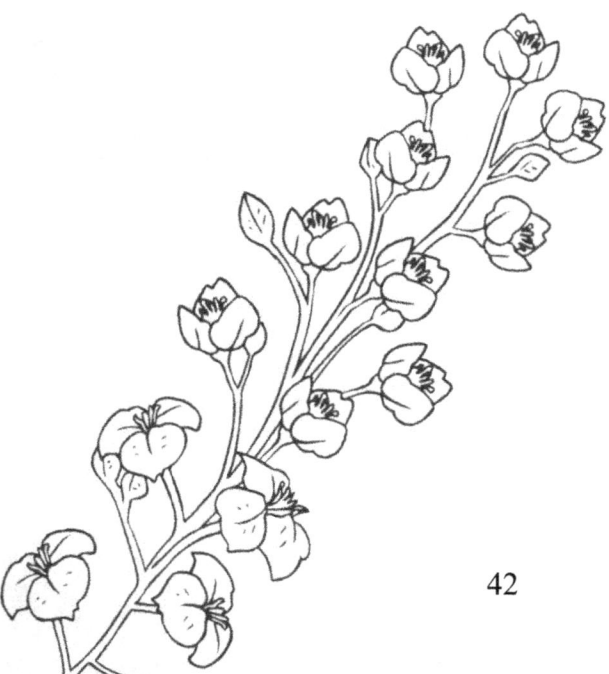

Forgive the old versions of yourself; you did not know the greatness deep inside of you. Forgive the girl or boy inside of you who was not aware and had not yet discovered who God designed you to be, the wonderfully created you.

Growth is taking place when you begin to recognize the gold inside of you that you have longed for others to see in you. See the gold inside of you and do not wait for others to see it.

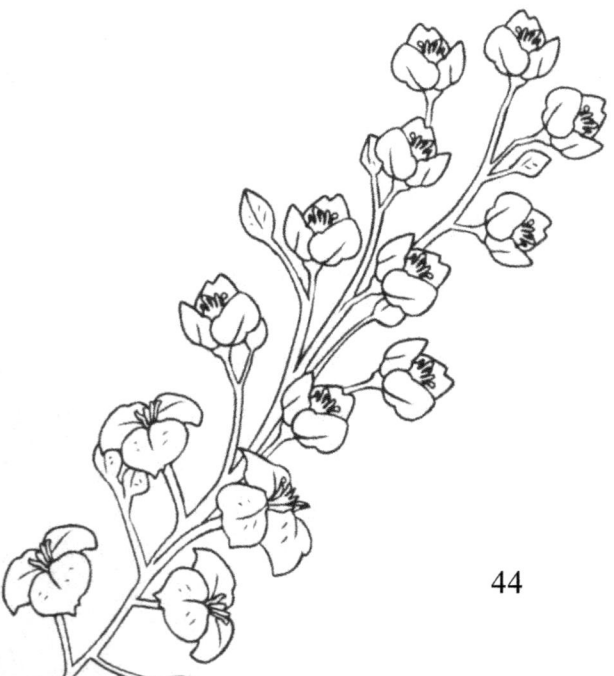

If you desire healing in any area of your life, identify an old thing that is a deterrent to the transformation you seek.

Life Is Full: Musings on the Beauty of Life, Growth, and Love

---

If you are not experiencing your heart's truest desires, evaluate what is taking its place and taking up space.

There are times when the most unexpected and unfortunate circumstances catapult us into another dimension of growth and evolution.

People will not value or honor who you are pretending to be. It is essential that you are fully who you are called to be. Be fierce. Once you know who you are and who you are called to be, never relinquish your crown.

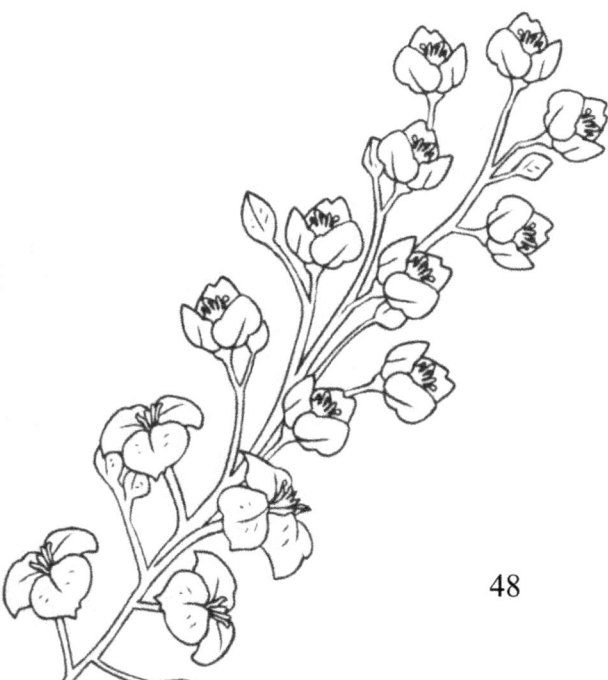

You are not your past errors. Your flawed past will never define you. We learn from flaws and we move past flaws.
Flaws are not to be worn, but rather should be used to grow and become more deeply rooted in who we truly are.

You will soon learn to leave things where they are. Do not force things that are stuck or misaligned to move along with you. You will recognize when the "who or what" that is unwilling or misaligned is you.

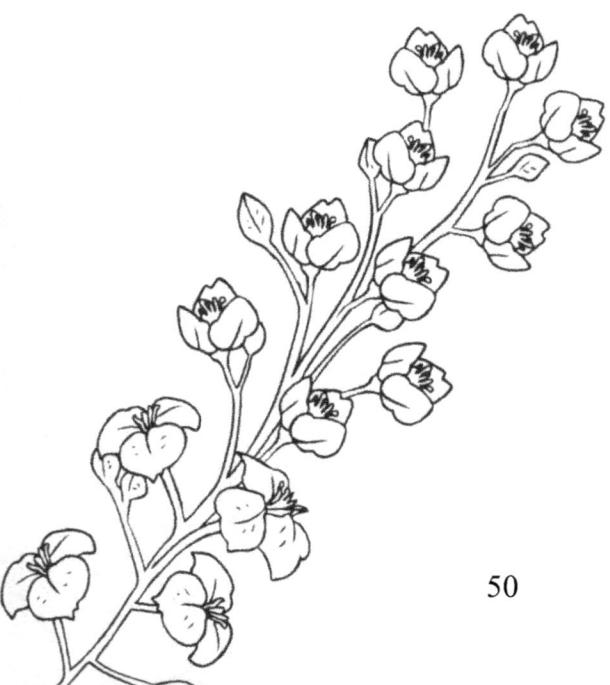

You will become more and more moved by compassion when you begin to see how we are all the same. We all have the same needs and wants, but it comes packed a little differently. You will see how we all need forgiveness; we all need and want love; we want to feel accepted and worthy. Compassion will grow in your heart when you recognize how much you, yourself, need it.

When you discover your gifts, you discover your lane, and you discover a garden that God has called *YOU* to cultivate. When good gardeners fall in love with their garden, they do not keep their attention on other people's gardens. Good gardeners become focused on their land and bringing forth whatever they are growing and harvesting. Fall in love with what God has given to you to grow and care for.

When you are committed to growth, you are committed to love. You are committed to loving yourself and to unlocking every gift and all of your potential.

Be honest, about everything.

Do not be so self-consumed, that you miss the moments others need you.

A sign of growth is when you decide to stop allowing your life to be a dumping ground or an abandoned lot where weeds grow and unwanted trash clutters—where otherwise good ground exists. Growth says, "No. Only good things grow here."

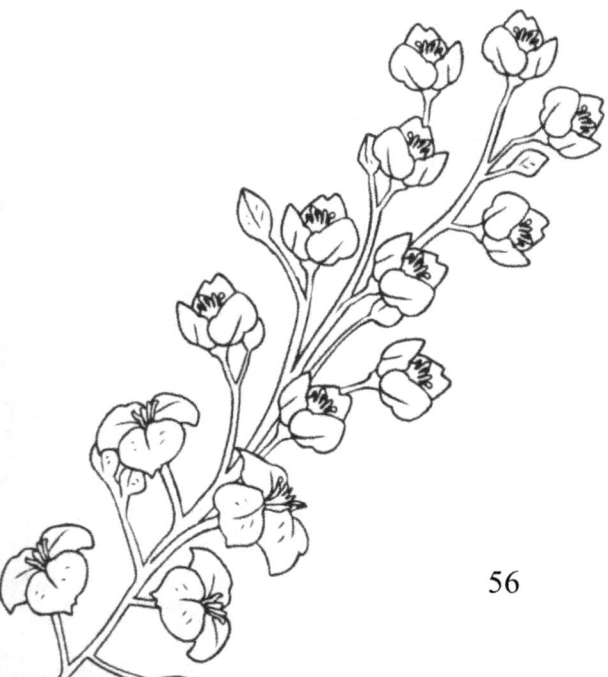

You will learn that what you possess can grow when you discover, learn, and use it. In discovering and using your gifts abundantly, you learn how to not only give thanks for your gifts but you will recognize and give thanks for the gifts of others. Discovering, cultivating, and mastering the gifts God has planted in us, indeed makes room for us to abundantly do more. Our gifts make room for us to not only do more but to become more and do more for others.

Every day we are building a life, beautiful or indifferent. Each day we are building a life and a legacy. We determine how our days will be read by our children and their children.

It is on the path of "trying" that you discover "you can."

Never try to convince others to stay in your life. Never persuade another to love you. You must be your biggest cheerleader and the one who loves you best. Always remember that we are each gradually evolving and adjusting to the paths of our lives.

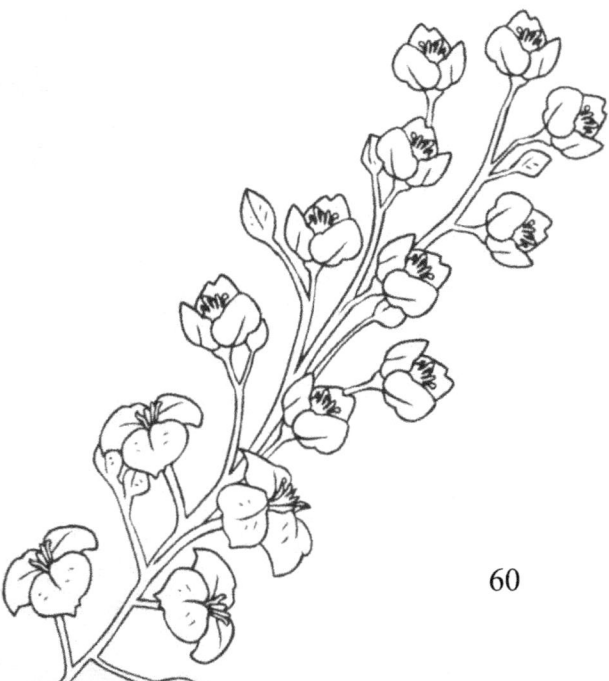

The beauty of growth is present when you place grace, gratitude, and goodness in front of any challenge that you are facing.

Defining your worth and value by who you were created to be and the purpose you were created for is far greater than any other measure.

Growth is when you stop looking for others to see greatness in you, and you recognize greatness within yourself.

Your confidence will grow; start by better managing your thoughts and your words about yourself and your life.

When you are called to greatness, you will have to be okay with being different, sometimes misunderstood and nonconforming to trends and what's considered average. You will have to be okay with not fitting in, but it's for a greater purpose. Greatness rarely fits in or looks like what's normal and average. Be okay with flowing upward even when it feels uncomfortable.

Fall in love with focus.
Focus on the One who matters above everything.
Focus on love and not small matters. Focus on the path
God has established for you.

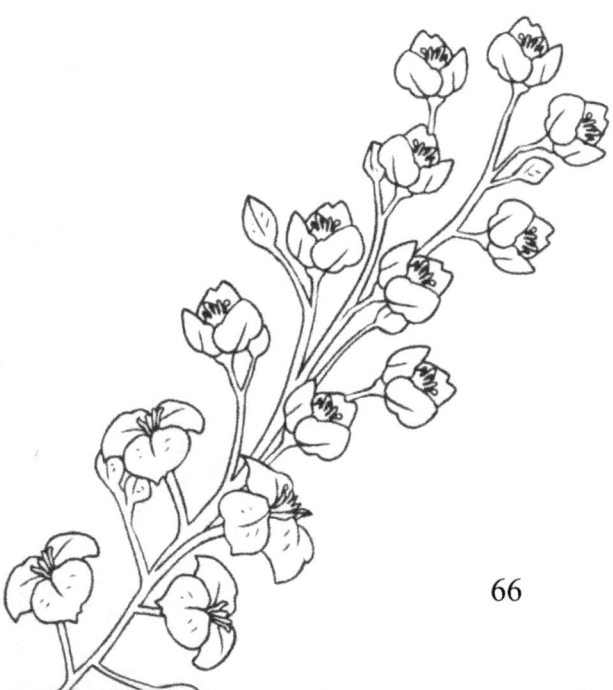

You will learn that your gifts are not only for you but for serving others. With understanding, your gifts will provide abundantly for you and others. Love, wisdom, and a heart like God's will be required to understand the power of your gifts and to understand that each of us is a gift planted in this world to produce good fruit.

Honoring the gifts inside of you, the gift of who you are, and making the most of your gifts will increase when you add joy and gratitude to it. Multiply what you have. You have a great gift inside of you. It was planted there from the beginning of time.

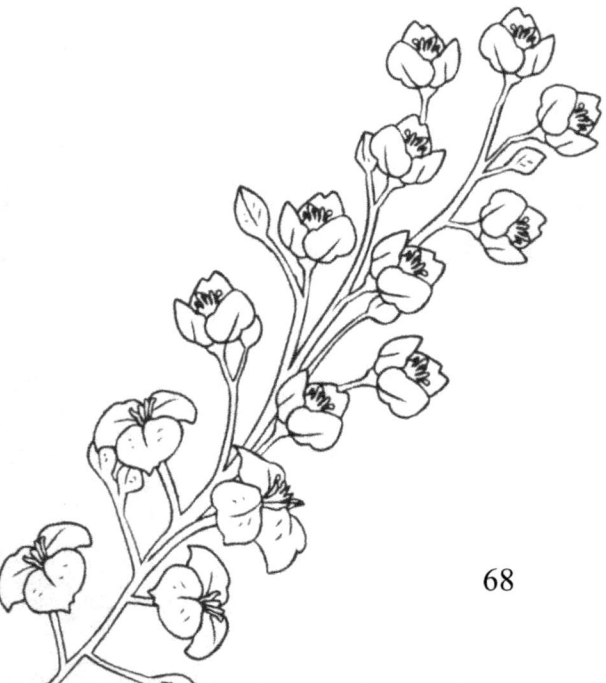

There is power in reclaiming your peace, your peacefulness, and being a peacemaker. Blessed are you when you unbox the gift of peace.

Being with yourself, as needed, is not loneliness. Creating a peaceful retreat for yourself to recharge is not isolation.

Growth is really liking yourself.
Growth is loving yourself.
Growth is truly accepting yourself.
Growth is love.
To not evolve is like denying yourself a gift.

If your life is not full of the outcomes and experiences that you desire, you must look at your patterns, your approaches, habits, and what has been your way of life. Your decisions and patterns are a result of what is filling your life.
Change something and grow.

Use your voice to express your standards and desires and then act accordingly. Advocate for yourself with precision and clarity.

Your actions are speaking what you actually believe. Be sure your actions, words, and thoughts are aligned with what you truly believe and what you desire.

If you do not honor yourself, love yourself, and regard yourself as royalty, what you believe will speak loudly to every room you enter and to every person you encounter. Be sure about who God has said you are and wear your crown well.

Life Is Full: Musings on the Beauty of Life, Growth, and Love

---

What we deeply believe spills out into our daily lives in ways we sometimes do not realize. What we believe about ourselves is sending that exact message to others and actualizing your experiences.

Rule your thoughts and perception, and you rule the outcomes of your life.

Check your internal message to yourself. What are you
thinking most of the time? What are you saying?
What you believe about yourself matters.

Friendship is beautiful. Friendship with others is a blessing. Friendship with yourself is even sweeter. Friendship with God is even greater.

Relationships are a great way to gauge your maturation. Some relationships become like crutches and support your remaining the same. Evaluate your relationships often.

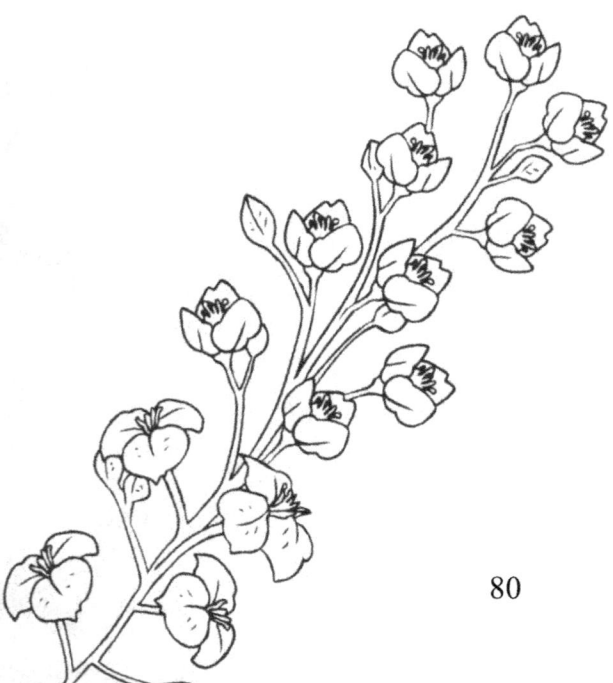

Never allow someone to guilt you into a decision. Only love should influence us.

Do your relationships challenge you? Or do they encourage your current mindsets, comfort zones, and applaud when you are not rising to your fullest potential? We crave comfort because it seems like safety from the unknown. Push forward and stay out of the comfort zone of remaining the same.

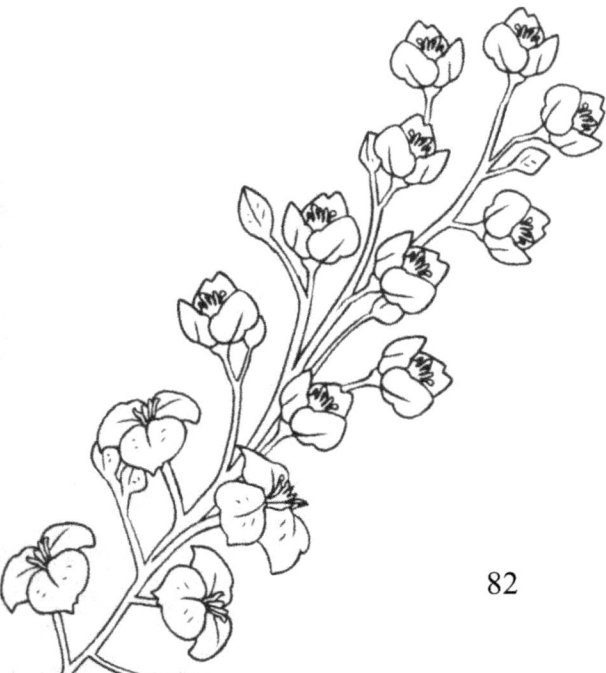

Relationships that don't challenge you to be great will soon become crutches that you rely upon. In your relationships, you should not always be the one who is right. You should not always be the one who knows it all. If your inadequacies are going unchecked, are you in a healthy and productive friendship?

First, check your relationship with yourself, and then you will discover why your relationships with others are what they are and what you have allowed them to be.

You will need trusted mentors and reliable close confidants to help train your character. Don't fight against it, embrace this as love.

Identifying unhealthy patterns in your life can empower you to break those patterns and create new patterns that not only change your life for the better but also change the generations that follow you and are learning from you.

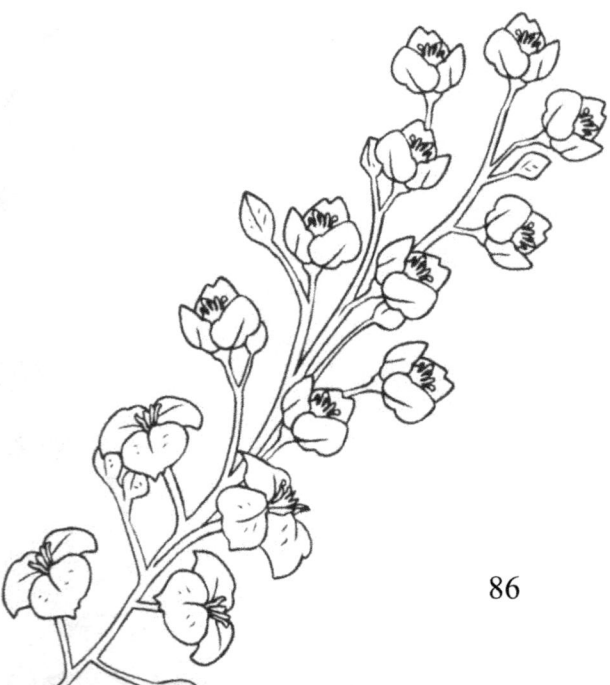

It is not necessary to always be available to others. Boundaries, priorities, and balance are essential. Sometimes love is expressed by refraining from being overwhelmed. We not only express love to ourselves in this way, but we create an example for others to see what love looks like.

Be brave. Be brave when facing the areas of your life that require change and be brave when facing transition. Fear keeps you in places of comfort. Courage pushes you to explore what is beyond your norm. Take courage and be open to transformation.

We should not hold a person hostage to their faults and flaws. Forgive them. Forgive them all. Many are not aware of their capacity to grow or to properly love another person because many do not know how to love themselves. Forgive them and move forward.

Pride prohibits you from living a great life and locks you out of abundance. Do not allow foolish ego or pride deter your growth.

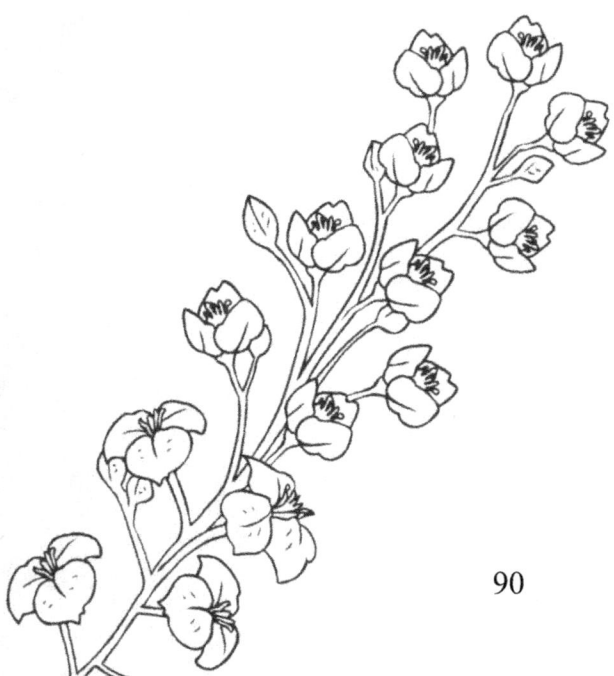

If you are carrying the weight of guilt or always feel as if you are wrong, this may be a sign that you need to release yourself from unnecessary requirements, pressures, and labels you have placed on yourself. It may also be a sign that you need peace from past mistakes. If there is a nagging presence of guilt in your life, it must be uprooted so that better things can grow in its place.

Your life is not a game, act accordingly.

No one can give you meaning or what you need, that you have not yet found inside yourself.

Live your vision, one step at a time.

Disagreement does not have to be contentious. Differences of opinion may lead to enlightenment. Grow upward.

It does not matter where you go. If you lack peace and happiness in your current state, a change of location will not always fix the problem. Discover joy where you are.

Beware of gray areas, they are the breeding grounds for
confusion and the eventual lie. Steer clear of gray areas,
especially when it comes to your values and the truth.
Either it is or it is not — that's clarity— knowing what is
and what is not.

The beauty of growing is being quick to check yourself, your heart, your motives, and your spirit before checking someone else's. This is the beauty of love in action.

Life is richer when we eliminate needless worries, distractions, and untruths.

Be who you are no matter where you are, what room you are in and regardless of the table where you are seated. Be you, but first know *who that is*.

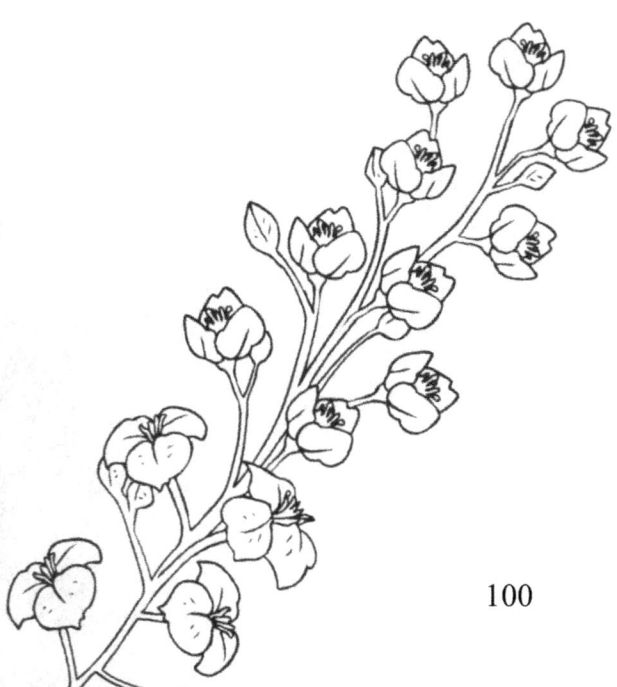

We need not rush any season of our lives. After all, we are being developed and fortified for an appointed time where our gifts will influence and impact others as God has designed. Until that appointed time, understand what you are now called to do and be.

We will never be able to escape from our personal responsibility to discover and live up to our fullest potential. Come what may and regardless of our starting points in life, how we finish will always matter.

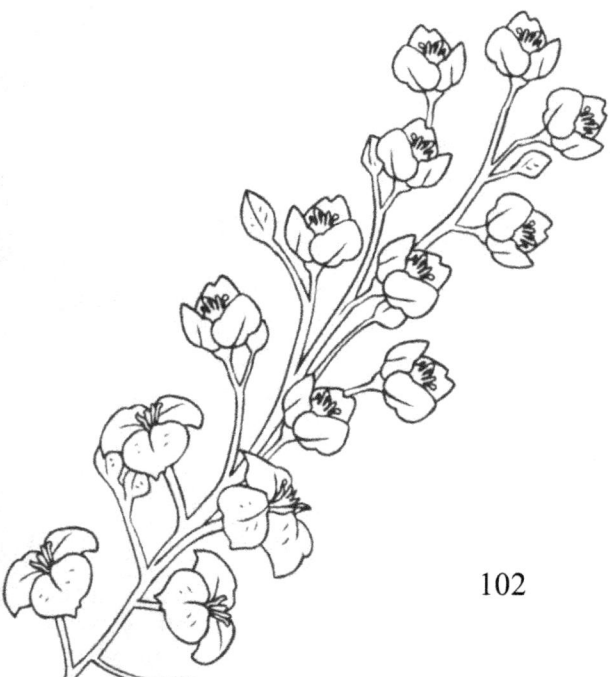

The Beauty of Love

THREE
THE BEAUTY OF LOVE

Like a garden, life is full of spaces available for growth and pruning. Life's seasons provide us with moments and memories that become ingrained in our hearts. There will be times of great challenge and times of great joy. At the core of life are beauty and the ability we have to grow and increase what is beautiful. The beauty of love working in us and through us is sometimes overlooked. Sometimes in life we are consumed with the busyness and what is not going as planned that we miss love at work around us. Life is full when we take time to celebrate, enjoy, be, and share love.

A fulfilled life is filled with contentment, compassion, and, in many ways, enjoying simplicity. Grasping the purpose for which you have been chosen is essential to understanding this gift you have been granted. Living a full life comes with growing in love and wisdom and the loving truth.

What do we make of the moments, the experiences, and the lessons in this life? What many consider as living is far beneath God's design. We are purpose-filled and purpose-destined souls created for a specific reason in the mind of our creator. Are we the God-designed fulfilling life as God has purposed? Our days should answer this question perpetually. Life is intended for more than merely existing and aimlessly wandering from experience to experience and from one moment to the next. Our unlimited, infinite and superabundantly creative God intended a way of life for His creation to experience and rule their space and time.

The beauty of love is knowing God. Knowing God is to truly know the beauty of love, because God is love. He is the originator and the place from which love flows.

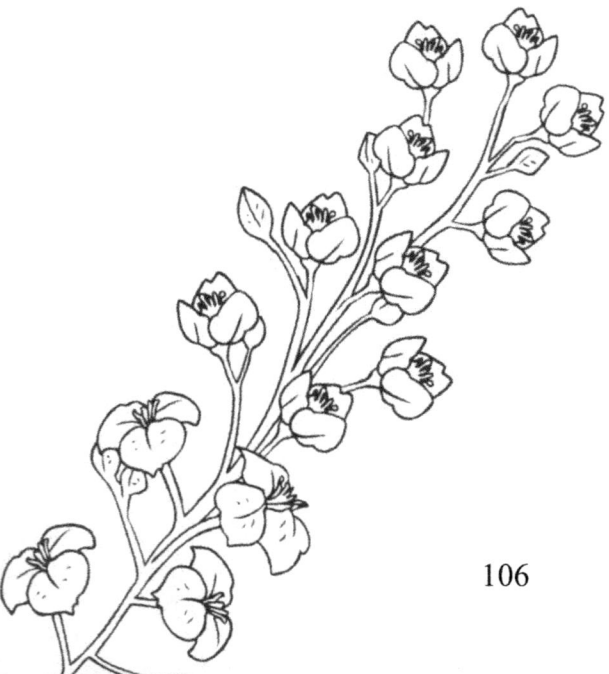

You will discover the greatest love when you discover the true definition of love. When you discover God is love, you will discover love in yourself. When you discover true love, you discover a greater level of clarity. You discover love in its truest and purest form. Once you find the true definition of love, you will learn to distinguish what isn't true love and what comes disguised as love.

Love is bold and courageous. It is unselfish. Love chooses you over and over again without fail. Love brings peace and is never a disruption.

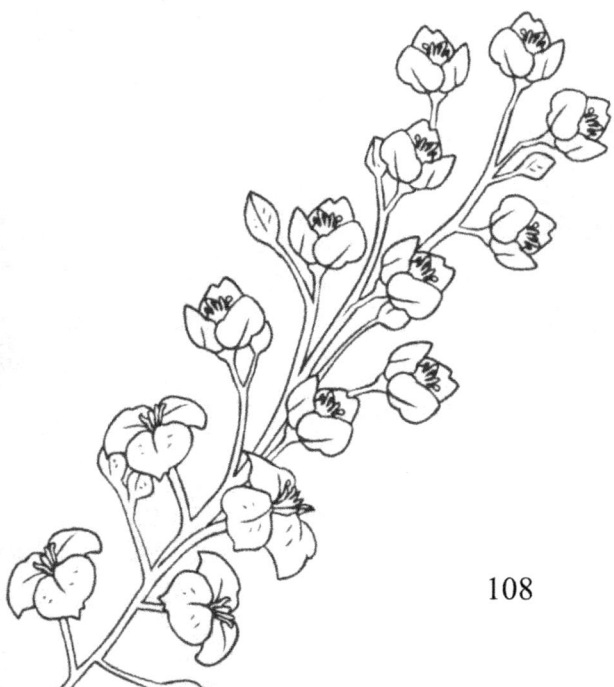

Love isn't lost. You grow in it. You discover love in yourself. Love has never been lost. We discover love in ourselves and we discover love in others. Essentially, we discover God in us and we discover God in others. God is love.

You are great because of what you possess in your soul;
God Himself handcrafted you.

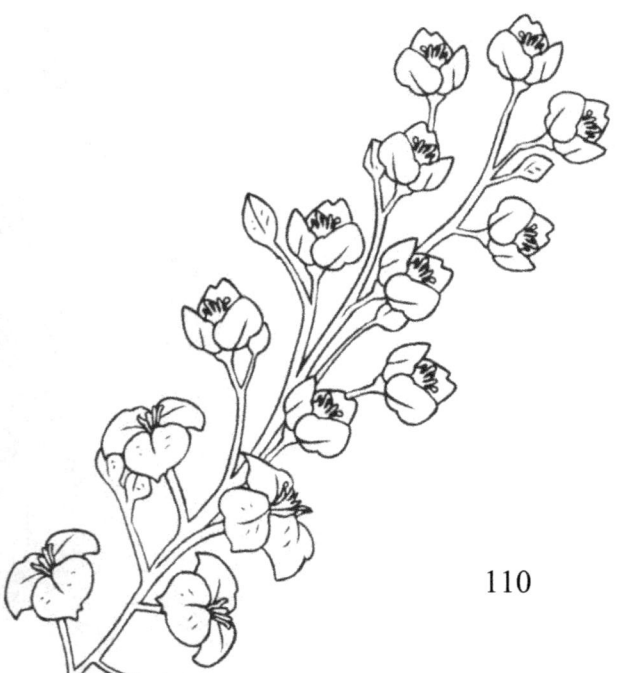

God is the ultimate power source - stay plugged in and connected.

Focus on your path, the one God has called you to walk.

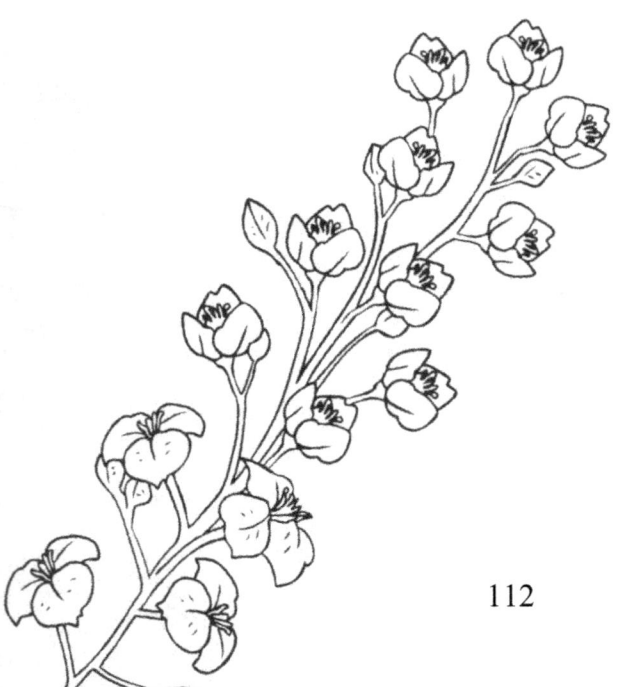

God's thoughts and desires are so far beyond what we can imagine. Don't create negative or contrary narratives and then say, "God has said it" to fit the reasons why some things are happening in your life. God is very loving and is fully aware of His great plans for you.

God in us and His hand mark upon us alone makes us far beyond average. Why would any God-made creation live below His design?

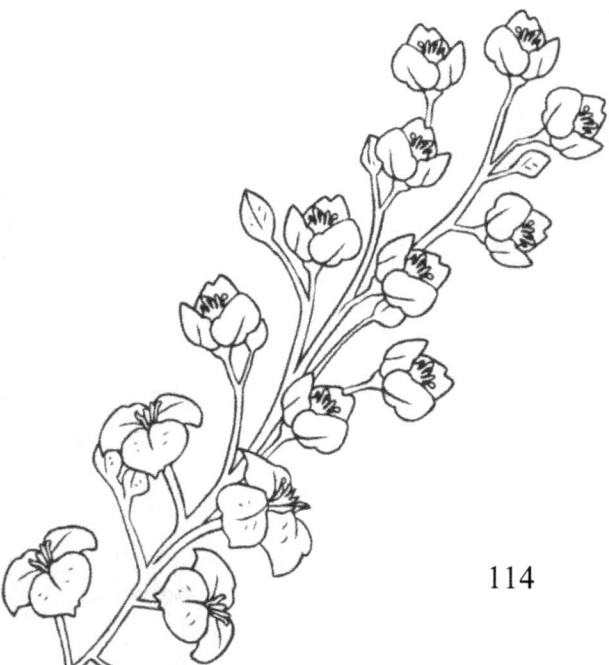

The more you realize how much you are experiencing God's grace and forgiveness, the more you grow to have compassion for others who have erred just as you have.

Do not rest in your insecurities, but acknowledge what they are so that they do not lead you.

Offer God your heart daily. Allow God into your heart. Be open and honest with God about the hard parts of your life and heart. Searching your heart for blockages leads to freedom from hindrance. Trust God with your heart. He knows how to handle you because He created you.

Being honest with God and with yourself about what is deeply buried in your heart liberates you. We cannot hide anything from Him; however we can be dishonest with ourselves, which ultimately draws us from the truth. Be liberated by being honest about what is in your heart and how it may be adding to or detracting from your life.

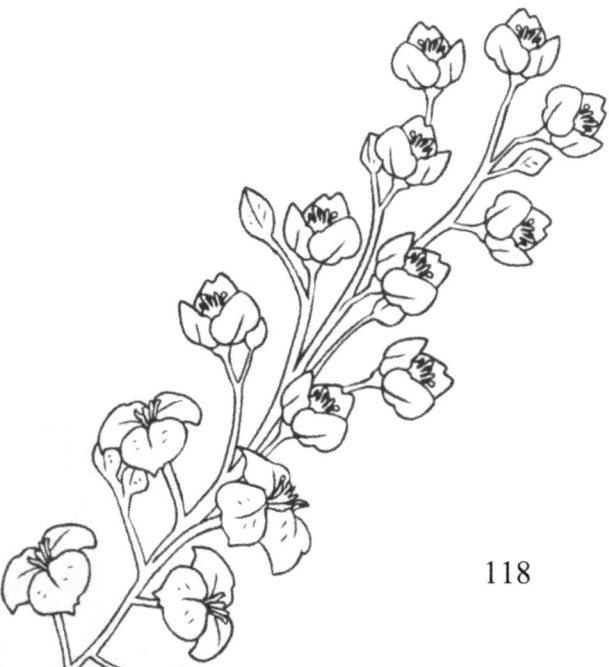

Do not wear labels that have not been divinely given to you. When you are not selected at a particular time or by a particular person that does not become a label you should own or wear. Not being selected for something does not exclude you from being chosen and purposed for something greater.

Not being selected by someone or for something usually indicates there is something more urgent that needs your attention. When others are selecting you, it means they are assigning you something to do that benefits their goals — and that is fine. However, there are times when your focus and attention need to be primarily channeled to accomplishing *your* goal. Choose yourself. Recognize when not being selected is a blessing and opportunity to advance your goals.

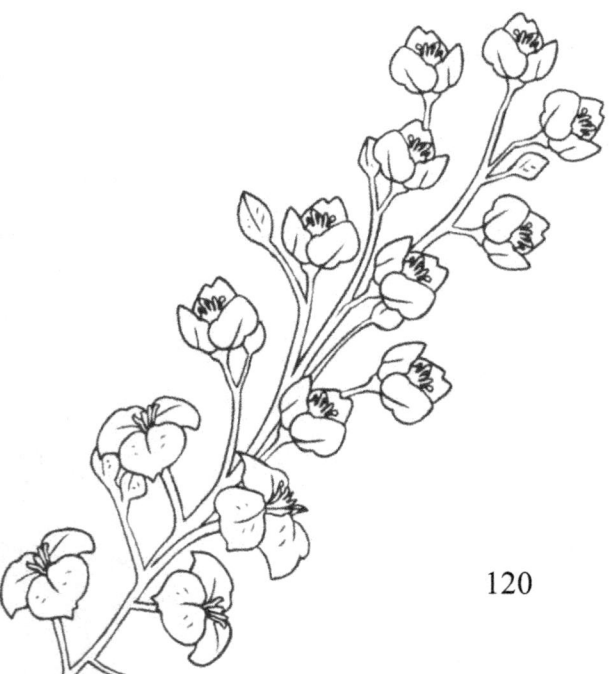

THE BEAUTY OF GOD

When we view our days as purposed and destined by God, we come to understand how rich our lives are with blessings. Life and its fullness are found in those quiet moments that overflow with peace and gratitude. The more we cherish and maximize our days that we are given the more we experience true purpose. The more we make good use of our days, the more we live out our purpose. Life is full of purpose. Life is full of goodness. Life is filled with opportunities for creating more life with the energy we put into what matters most.

With God and His Spirit living inside of us, we discover daily how to count our days by prioritizing what is beautiful, whole, and loving. Even our darkest hours become a catalyst that propels us to a deeper understanding of our purpose and allows us to transcend what may have betrayed our trust and hopes. *Life is so full.* It is full of beautiful moments to discover power and the truth of God's purpose for us. Life is not defined by low moments but by how we rise above them and use those moments to produce something greater than what was experienced. In a lifetime we are presented with many opportunities to co-create with God.

How do you measure the days you have been given and the moments that God has given to you? How do we love God, ourselves, and others? How do we navigate the space between physical birth and physical death? We do so by viewing life as full of robust moments that are filled with opportunities to achieve one's God-designed purpose.

To know God is to know yourself.
To discover His character and His voice is life.
Life is full of God's purpose on display and in active motion.
To love God is to love yourself, His creation.
Look at yourself and praise God for the beauty of His work and the creation He made in you.

Your posture, confidence, and approach to life changes when you acknowledge that you are God's purpose in living form.

The beauty of love is first knowing that God is love.
God is the giver of this gift.
Seeing God in yourself is to recognize love inside of you.
Seeking love should lead us to discovering God.

Agreement with God causes the soul to flourish.
Agreement with God and His thoughts about you mutes every message in conflict with God's good thoughts toward you.
Agree with God with your entire heart.
Agree with God.

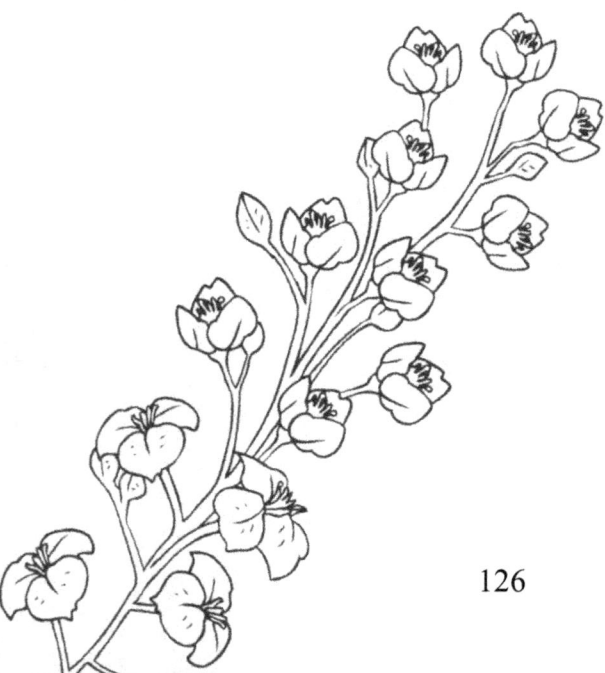

Discovering your God-designed self is a beautiful experience. To discover who God says we are is the process of becoming aware of who we were always purposed to be. Interestingly, in this process there are many outside influences that attempt to infiltrate this grand design we are created to live in. Everything changes the moment you embrace the you designed by God. Your vision, your approach, your posture, and how you allow yourself to be positioned in the world drastically changes.

This belief must be fixed in our minds and planted deeply in our hearts: God does not perform or bring harm to us; He only has plans to care for us and to cause us to flourish. When this is fixed in our hearts, we will conquer opposition and approach challenges with a winning mindset. God will not abandon you. Only place confidence in God.

Your life is not a game of chance to God. God has a well thought out plan that is worth embracing.

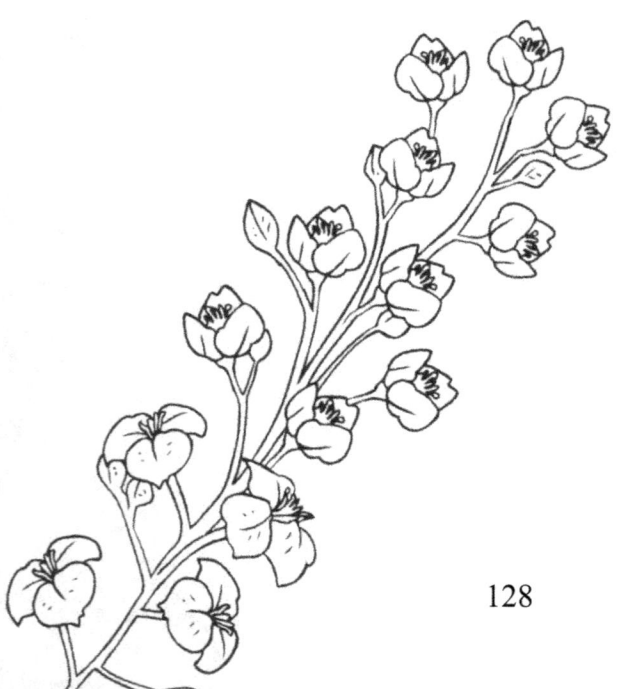

You are made in God's likeness; live as such. To live in His likeness is to come to know God. Living in His image is recognizing your divine makeup and capacity that goes beyond this earthly realm.

God is not what so many have made Him out to be. God is so very much beyond what humans can fathom. Do not limit your experience with God based on the limited minds of people. God and His excellence are endlessly expansive. Abandon your definition of who God has been based on limitations or misfortunes you have experienced and explore who God is daily by discovering and experiencing Him through His Living Spirit and Living Word. We must experience God intimately.

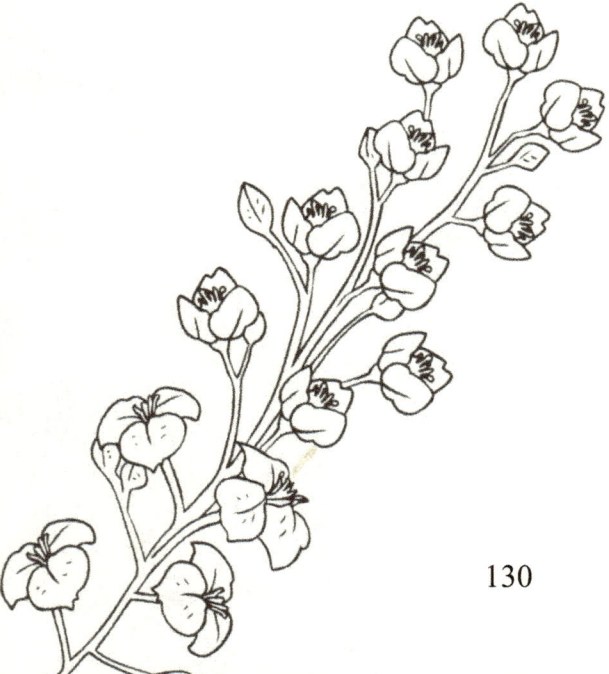

Honoring the gift of God in you can take many forms: discovering and maintaining a vision for your life; discovering and prioritizing your purpose; caring for your life and for your temple. Honoring the gift of your life also includes obeying God, planning for your life, and caring well for the resources God brings into your life. Cultivating a beautiful life is honoring God.

Success is prioritizing God over everything.

Never believe the lie that God does not care for you.
Never believe that you are forgotten; you certainly are not.
God deeply cares for you; believe that.

Life is full of goodness and opportunities to increase what we have been given, over and over again. Life is beautiful and not difficult to navigate when we find definition in God's master design. There is great peace in discovering and pursuing heavenly wisdom pertaining to this life assignment.

To love God is to honor who He has called you to be. To love God is to honor the purpose you were created for. To love God is to love Him in yourself and to love Him in others.

Life is full when we discover and engage the power of love. Life is full when we perpetually grow. Life is awaiting you to make the most of it.

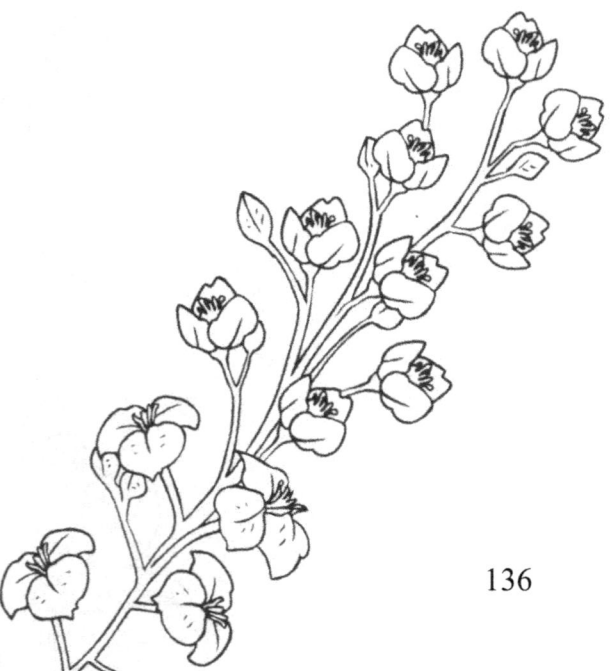

CLOSING REFLECTIONS

Our lives reflect what is deep in our souls, our thoughts, hearts, and in our hopes. What is in your soul today? What do you want to reside in your soul--in your mind--that leads you to live a fulfilled life?

Each day unfolds with outcomes we either planned for or did not plan for. Yet, there remains a level of ownership. We have to multiply the good that we possess in our souls. Living, truly experiencing this life as God desires us to, is to give attention to what produces more life, such as peace that exceeds our expectations; hope that continually believes in the best of things; and love that gives birth to forgiveness and freedom. A full heart causes us to see beyond momentary disappointments and misunderstandings, and we draw wisdom and growth from these times. As we treasure the gifts that we are and take notice of the gifts in others, we grasp the importance and power of love and how it helps us grow. A fulfilling life is unfolding daily as we give attention to the greatness God has planted inside of us. That greatness, that every God-created individual has, is meant to grow, to be cultivated, and shared throughout their days.

We each have a decision to live a full life or to not experience a full life. The choice of our heart reflects our decision by the path we choose. Will the garden that is our life produce beautiful things, generational blessings and greatness, or will it become an abandoned dirt lot that gathers regrets, fear, and serves as the dumping ground for poor choices and lack of cultivation. Many land lots once used as illegal trash dumps have been turned into thriving gardens that serve cities and communities for years beyond even the life of the one who started the garden. Sadly, many beautiful gardens are abandoned when the caretaker stops investing in and maintaining the land. Then, there are gardeners who find a lot of land, and they consistently tend to their garden day after day, planting, pulling up weeds, watering, harvesting and repeating this process year after year. The latter gardener recognizes not only how valuable land is, but what it can be used for to produce abundance. This same gardener sees the value in how it will feed her family, her community, and how her actions will teach her children to invest time in attention to cultivating such a beautiful and important land.

This principle applies to life. We cultivate our lives by the attention and investments we make in ourselves; our vision, and to a legacy that will serve others in future generations. Life is opportunity. We have daily opportunities to show up greater and greater and to thrive beyond any conditions ever presented to us.

To love life is to grow it and to view it as a most precious gift. Experiencing God in our days forever changes how we experience love with ourselves and others.

If your life is not flourishing, the good news is that just as you can turn unused land into a thriving garden, so can you turn your life into a thriving one. This is the beauty of God and His creative power that works in each of us. One epic idea, a shift in perspective, birthing something divine and beautiful out of a chapter of great turmoil is where spiritual and personal transformation can happen. Life should not dictate to us the quality of our days, but rather we should with our actions, our thoughts, our words, our beliefs create a life that we love and desire to live.

Each of us must define how a full life looks. Hopefully that definition is well aligned by the life God always intended and desired for you to experience. It is a life where love is the priority; wisdom is a necessity, and where we pursue and attain peace daily. Life is full when our souls are prospering.

May the reflections of my life and the lessons I have learned and continue to learn reach your heart. May we learn daily to renew our minds and soak ourselves in God's great love. May we then share that same love with others as we shed past experiences that may be daunting.

May we embrace the beauty of God's power that is available to us when we accept and believe His plan for us which was spoken before the worlds were created. Life is full because we embrace the purpose we were created for and He who created us.

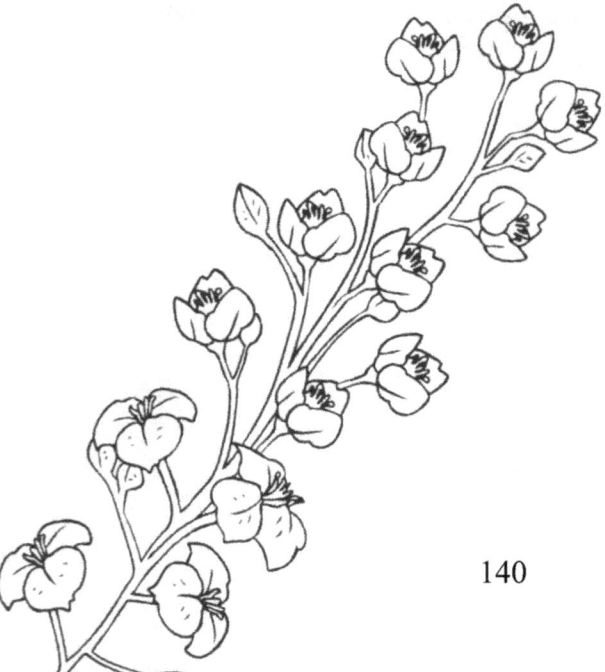

ABOUT THE AUTHOR

Cassandra is an emerging thought leader poised to reach millions of readers experiencing life transitions with a message of hope and transformational insight on shifting and elevating mindsets and personal vision to experience fulfilled living. Cassandra desires to support others as they embrace their God-design.

Cassandra N. Vincent is a certified personal and executive coach and transformational speaker on a mission to lead a movement of happy and whole women who are committed to leading with purpose and living the life they desire. Driven by her personal story of challenge and triumph, her messages are soaked in themes of empowerment, personal development and growth. She holds a Bachelor of Science degree in Business Administration from Morgan State University (2004) and a Personal and Executive Coaching certificate from The CAPP Institute (2018).

Cassandra is a dynamic communicator who speaks from a place of compassion, transparency, and authenticity, making her an in-demand speaker and facilitator.

Thanks to her unique ability to help audiences change the way they see themselves and their lives, Cassandra's talks and signature event, "The Vision +

Strategy Brunch" are truly transformational. Her gift lies in helping women create a vision for their lives.

Cassandra is the author of *The Smart Woman's Bounce Back Guide After a Bad Breakup* **and** *Vision+Strategy Workbook: A Reflection Guide for the Woman Who Is Ready to Change Her World.*

Cassandra and her boxer pup, MaxChester, live in Maryland.

ABOUT THE BOOK

Life is Full: Musings on the Beauty of Life, Growth, and Love, is a collection of Cassandra N. Vincent's reflections. As a lover of the power of understanding one's purpose, Cassandra is sharing nuggets of wisdom in *Life is Full* to encourage anyone who either needs a powerful reminder of the gift that life is or for anyone who enjoys thoughtful reflection. This book comes as a preface to the author's entering a new phase of life and celebrates all of the transitioning and personal transformation that she has undergone. *Life is Full* is a celebratory reflection of what was, what is, and what is to come. She encourages approaching the future with a clear vision, deep grasp of purpose, and discovery of one's God-designed self. Readers will enjoy enriching reflections and thought-provoking sentiments that will prompt them to pause and reflect. *Life is Full* is an exhibit of affirmations and reflections of culminating moments.

www.ingramcontent.com/pod-product-compliance
Lightning Source LLC
Chambersburg PA
CBHW031356040426
42444CB00005B/313